BRIGHT DEAD THINGS

ALSO BY ADA LIMÓN

Lucky Wreck

This Big Fake World

Sharks in the Rivers

BRIGHT DEAD THINGS

———

POEMS BY

ADA LIMÓN

MILKWEED EDITIONS

Published 2015 by Milkweed Editions
Printed in the United States of America
Cover design by Gretchen Achilles
Author photo by Jude Domski

23 24 25 26 27   19 18 17 16 15
SECOND EDITION

Milkweed Editions, an independent nonprofit publisher, gratefully acknowledges sustaining support from
the Lindquist & Vennum Foundation; the McKnight Foundation; the National Endowment for the Arts;
the Target Foundation; and other generous contributions from foundations, corporations, and individu-
als. Also, this activity is made possible by the voters of Minnesota through a Minnesota State Arts Board
Operating Support grant, thanks to a legislative appropriation from the arts and cultural heritage fund, and
a grant from the Wells Fargo Foundation Minnesota. For a full listing of Milkweed Editions supporters,
please visit milkweed.org.

Library of Congress Cataloging-in-Publication Data

Limón, Ada.
  [Poems. Selections]
  Bright dead things / Ada Limón. -- First edition.
     pages cm
  ISBN 978-1-57131-471-0 (alk. paper) -- ISBN 978-1-57131-925-8 (ebook)
  I. Title.
  PS3612.I496A6 2015
  811'.6--dc23
                                                          2015000088

Milkweed Editions is committed to ecological stewardship. We strive to align our book production
practices with this principle, and to reduce the impact of our operations in the environment. We are a mem-
ber of the Green Press Initiative, a nonprofit coalition of publishers, manufacturers, and authors working
to protect the world's endangered forests and conserve natural resources. *Bright Dead Things* was printed on
acid-free 100% postconsumer-waste paper by McNaughton & Gunn.

For Lucas & Lily Bean

CONTENTS

4:

Who among the numberless you have become desires this moment

Which comprehends nothing more than loss & fragility & the fleeing of flesh?

—LARRY LEVIS

I

I like the lady horses best,
how they make it all look easy,
like running 40 miles per hour
is as fun as taking a nap, or grass.
I like their lady horse swagger,
after winning. Ears up, girls, ears up!
But mainly, let's be honest, I like
that they're ladies. As if this big
dangerous animal is also a part of me,
that somewhere inside the delicate
skin of my body, there pumps
an 8-pound female horse heart,
giant with power, heavy with blood.
Don't you want to believe it?
Don't you want to lift my shirt and see
the huge beating genius machine
that thinks, no, it knows,
it's going to come in first.

1.

There are so many people who've come before us,
arrows and wagon wheels, obsidian tools, buffalo.
Look out at the meadow, you can almost see them,
generations dissolved in the bluegrass and hay.
I want to try and be terrific. Even for an hour.

2.

If you walk long enough, your crowded head clears,
like how all the cattle run off loudly as you approach.
This fence is a good fence, but I doubt my own haywire
will hold up to all this blank sky, so open and explicit.
I'm like a fence, or a cow, or that word, *yonder.*

3.

There is a slow tractor traffic hollering outside,
and I'd like not to be traffic, but the window shaking.
Your shoes are piled up with mine, and the heat
comes on, makes a simple noise, a dog-yawn.
People have done this before, but not us.

It was only months when it felt like I had been
washing the dishes forever.

Hardwood planks under the feet, a cord to the sky.
What is it to go to a *We* from an *I*?

Each time he left for an errand, the walls
would squeeze me in. I cried over the nonexistent bathmat, wet
   floor of him,
how south we were, far away in the outskirts.

(All the new bugs.)

I put my apron on as a joke and waltzed around carrying
a zucchini like a child.

This is Kentucky, not New York, and I am not important.

This was before we got the dog even, and before I trusted
the paralyzing tranquilizer of love stuck
in the flesh of my neck.

Back home, in my apartment, another woman lived there.
In Brooklyn, by the deli, where everything
was clean and contained.

(Where I grieved my deaths.)

I took to my hands and knees. I was thinking about the novel
I was writing. The great heavy chest of live animals
I had been dragging around for years; what's life?

I made the house so clean (shine and shine and shine).

I was suspicious of the monkey sounds of Kentucky's birds,
judging crackles, rusty mailbox, spiders in the magnolia tree,
tornado talk, dead June bugs like pinto beans.

Somewhere I had heard that, after noting the lack
of water pressure in an old hotel in Los Angeles,
they found a woman's body at the bottom
of the cistern.

Imagine, just thinking the water was low, just wanting
to take a shower.

After that, when the water would act weird,
spurt, or gurgle, I'd imagine a body, a woman, a me
just years ago, freely single, happily unaccounted for,
at the lowest curve of the water tower.

Yes, and over and over,
I'd press her limbs down with a long pole
until she was still.

The man across the street is mowing 40 acres on a small lawn mower. It's so small, it must take him days, so I imagine that he likes it. He must. He goes around each tree carefully. He has 10,000 trees; it's a tree farm, so there are so many trees. One circle here. One circle there. My dog and I've been watching. The light's escaping the sky, and there's this place I like to stand, it's before the rise, so I'm invisible. I'm standing there, and I've got the dog, and the man is mowing in his circles. So many circles. There are no birds or anything, or none that I can see. I imagine what it must be like to stay hidden, disappear in the dusky nothing and stay still in the night. It's not sadness, though it may sound like it. I'm thinking about people and trees and how I wish I could be silent more, be more tree than anything else, less clumsy and loud, less crow, more cool white pine, and how it's hard not to always want something else, not just to let the savage grass grow.

What should we believe in next?

Daniel Boone's brother's grave says, *Killed by Indians.*

     We point at it; poke at it like a wound—
              history's noose.

Below the grave, a cold spring runs.
     Clear, like a conscience.

     Now, I'm alone.

     Only me and the white bones of an animal's hand
     revealed in the silt.

There remains the mystery of how the pupil devours
so much bastard beauty. Abandoned property.

This land and I are rewilding.

A bird I don't know but follow with my still-living eye.

The day before me undresses in the wet southern heat—
       flower mouth,
       pollen burn,
       wing sweat.

I don't want to be only the landscape: the bone's buried.

Let the subject be
> the movement of the goldenrod, the mustard,
> the cardinal, the jay, the generosity.

I don't want anything,
not even to show it to you—

> the beak grass, bottlebrush, dandelion seed head,
> parachute and crown,
> all the intention of wishes, forgiveness,

this day's singular existence in time,
the native field flourishing selfishly, only for itself.

A bat cracks in the flickering background
and we're dead tired from the horse track,
all those losing bets stuck crumpled up
in our cheap fedoras, but no one, not even
the dog, is unhappy. Baseball announcers
are trying to be funny about nothing, crowds
cheer on the momentum of the home team
and it's not too early for pj's, or promises,
or some low-sung lullaby that salutes
the original songs on the inside. I decide,
someday, to name a kid Levon, and you
agree, and outside the dark traffic groans by
on our curving country road making a sound
like the slow roar of applause when
the home team's tide unexpectedly turns.

The dog does this beautiful thing,
it waits. It stills itself and determines
that the waiting is essential.

I suppose this eternity
is the one inside the drawer,
inside the buttonhole.

All the shouting before
was done out loud, on the street,
and now it's done so shushing-ly.

There is a saying down here,
I'd never heard before,
I hate it for you.

It means, if the dog pees
on the carpet, *I hate it
for you, Too bad for you.*

It means, if you're alone,
when love is all around,
*We all tip our lonely hats
in one un-lonely sound.*

So we might understand each other better:
I'm leaning on the cracked white window ledge
in my nice pink slippers lined with fake pink fur.
The air conditioning is sensational. Outside,
we've put up a cheap picnic table beneath the maple
but the sun's too hot to sit in, so the table glows
on alone like bleached-out bones in the heat.
Yesterday, so many dead in Norway. Today,
a big-voiced singer found dead in her London flat.
And this country's gone standstill and criminal.
I want to give you something, or I want to take
something from you. But I want to feel the exchange,
the warm hand on the shoulder, the song coming out
and the ear holding on to it. Maybe we could meet
at that table under the tree, just right out there.
I'm passing the idea to you in this note:
the table, the tree, the pure heat of late July.
We could be in that same safe place watching
the sugar maple throw down its winged seeds
like the tree wants to give us something too—
some sweet goodness that's so hard to take.

I'm learning so many different ways to be quiet. There's how I stand in the lawn, that's one way. There's also how I stand in the field across from the street, that's another way because I'm farther from people and therefore more likely to be alone. There's how I don't answer the phone, and how I sometimes like to lie down on the floor in the kitchen and pretend I'm not home when people knock. There's daytime silent when I stare, and a nighttime silent when I do things. There's shower silent and bath silent and California silent and Kentucky silent and car silent and then there's the silence that comes back, a million times bigger than me, sneaks into my bones and wails and wails and wails until I can't be quiet anymore. That's how this machine works.

I haven't given up on trying to live a good life,
a really good one even, sitting in the kitchen
in Kentucky, imagining how agreeable I'll be—
the advance of fulfillment, and of desire—
all these needs met, then unmet again.
When I was a kid, I was excited about carrots,
their spidery neon tops in the garden's plot.
And so I ripped them all out. I broke the new roots
and carried them, like a prize, to my father
who scolded me, rightly, for killing his whole crop.
I loved them: my own bright dead things.
I'm thirty-five and remember all that I've done wrong.
Yesterday I was nice, but in truth I resented
the contentment of the field. Why must we practice
this surrender? What I mean is: there are days
I still want to kill the carrots because I can.

The tree comes to me
for the first time in weeks.
When did all its colors,
like some commercial for dying,
start shooting out of its skin?
This morning, we fucked
each other into a regular
backyard bonfire—cold wood
turned to coal in the fine,
fine flame. And now, this tree
breaks into view, lurid red leaves
that demand a clanging,
screaming alarm, and I think—
this tree has been here
all this time, and I didn't notice.
I swear, I'll try harder not to
miss as much: the tree, or how
your fingers under still
sleep-stunned sheets
coaxed all my colors back.

For Trish

Now when I go to the grocery store,
I'm amazed at the wide aisles of bright
food and food-stuffs, and it's nothing like
the bodega I shopped in for years,
in Brooklyn, between the bars we liked.
Once, when I was going for groceries,
I ran into T, and we decided we needed
to drink rather than shop, and we did.

There were a lot of beers on tap,
and the taps were all different like toys
in a dentist's toy chest, so I said,
I'll have what she's having,
and maybe it was snowing out,
and it seemed to be at a time when
every shirt I bought at the secondhand store
would turn out to be see-through,
but I wouldn't know it until I was out.
So, a lot of conversations would start,
Is this shirt see-through? And it was.

We talked for a long time, grocery bags
empty on the chair, and we both talked about
moving to someplace like Montana
and how sometimes it would be nice
to see more sky than just this little square
between the bridges and buildings,
but then we'd miss Brooklyn, and each other,
and we ordered another beer.

T was writing a play, also some articles,
and we both just needed some money,
and maybe to make out with someone
who wasn't an asshole. But also, we wanted
to make great art. T was really good at naming
things so we decided she should be a *Titleologist*
and she liked that, so she agreed.

What would we do if we lived in
someplace like Montana?

We'd go for walks, and look at trees,
and write and look at the sky.

Yes, and we'd cook and go to those huge grocery stores
that have toy cars attached to the carts so kids
can pretend to be driving.

Yes, and we'd probably have kids, too.

All of this seemed really far off and not like us at all,
so we ordered another beer and said, *Life is long.*

Now, I'm walking around the grocery store
in Kentucky and I've just looked at trees, and sky,
and I should write something, so I ask T to tell me
what to write about, she says, *Saturation*, and I think
of that feeling when you're really full, or life is full
and you can't think of anything else that could fit in it,

but then even more sky comes and more days
and there is so much to remember and swallow.
I ask T what I should call the thing I write about
Saturation, because she's a titleologist, and she says,
Someplace Like Montana.

Confession: I did not want to live here,
not among the goldenrod, wild onions,
or the dropseed, not waist-high in the barrel-
aged brown corn water, not with the million-
dollar racehorses, nor the tightly wound
round hay bales. Not even in the old tobacco
weigh station we live in, with its heavy metal
safe doors that frame our bricked bedroom
like the mouth of a strange beast yawning
to suck us in, each night, like air. I denied it,
this new land. But love, I'll concede this:
whatever state you are, I'll be that state's bird,
the loud, obvious blur of song people point to
when they wonder where it is you've gone.

Six horses died in a tractor-trailer fire.
There. That's the hard part. I wanted
to tell you straight away so we could
grieve together. So many sad things,
that's just one on a long recent list
that loops and elongates in the chest,
in the diaphragm, in the alveoli. What
is it they say, *heartsick* or *downhearted*?
I picture a heart lying down on the floor
of the torso, pulling up the blankets
over its head, thinking this pain will
go on forever (even though it won't).
The heart is watching Lifetime movies
and wishing, and missing all the good
parts of her that she has forgotten.
The heart is so tired of beating
herself up, she wants to stop it still,
but also she wants the blood to return,
wants to bring in the thrill and wind of the ride,
the fast pull of life driving underneath her.
What the heart wants? The heart wants
her horses back.

I used to pretend to believe in God. Mainly, I liked so much to talk to someone in the dark. Think of how far a voice must have to travel to go beyond the universe. How powerful that voice must be to get there. Once in a small chapel in Chimayo, New Mexico, I knelt in the dirt because I thought that's what you were supposed to do. That was before I learned to harness that upward motion inside me, before I nested my head in the blood of my body. There was a sign and it said, *This earth is blessed. Do not play in it.* But I swear I will play on this blessed earth until I die. I relied on a Miracle Fish, once, in New York City, to tell me my fortune. That was before I knew it was my body's water that moved it, that the massive ocean inside me was what made the fish swim.

This is the cooling part of the fever,
when everything: the jumping girder
of the Golden Gate's red limb, the tall
metal tree house of the Empire State,
the black rock cliffs off the Sonoma coast,
the drawer's leftover pills, the careless
cut, the careening car, the crosswalk,
the stop/go, the give up, give up, done,
all of it, slows to a real nice drive by. A view
of some tree breathing and the mind's wheels
ease up on the pavement's tug. That tree,
that one willowy thing over there,
can save a life, you know? It saves
by not trying, a leaf like some note
slipped under the locked blue door
(bathtub full, despair's drunk),
a small live letter that says only, *Stay*.

WHAT IT LOOKS LIKE TO US
AND THE WORDS WE USE

All these great barns out here in the outskirts,
black creosote boards knee-deep in the bluegrass.
They look so artfully abandoned, even in use.
You say they look like arks after the sea's
dried up, I say they look like pirate ships,
and I think of that walk in my valley where
J said, *You don't believe in God?* And I said,
No. I believe in this connection we all have
to nature, to each other, to the universe.
And she said, *Yeah, God.* And how we stood there,
low beasts among the white oaks, Spanish moss,
and spider webs, obsidian shards stuck in our pockets,
woodpecker flurry, and I refused to call it so.
So instead, we looked up at the unruly sky,
its clouds in simple animal shapes we could name
though we knew they were really just clouds—
disorderly, and marvelous, and ours.

2

BELLOW

Tell the range and all that's howling,
the flickers of life beyond the weeds,
the vulture's furrowed brow of flight,
the blasted sticky Canadian lawn thistle;
tell the clowned-out clouds and the rain,
and all that makes you go quiet again,
tell them that you didn't come here
to make a fuss, or break, or growl, or
scream; tell them—crazy sky and stars
between—tell them you didn't come
to disturb the night air and throw a fit,
then get down in the dark and do it.

I'm afraid that I won't do the right thing
in the face of disaster.

Or, I'm afraid I will be stupidly brave.

      I'll pull the helmet off the fallen when you're supposed
to leave it on, in case it's holding things together.

Also, I like to discuss my feelings too much.

The only thing I've learned about a home death
is that it requires a lot of washcloths.

*

When we started to make a home together,
he liked a lot of washcloths,
the small, cheap kind
for every day you're alive.

Sometimes I would have dreams
that she was still alive, and I couldn't find
enough washcloths to help her,
to clean her face,
the tumor's foul, black spit-up.

I'd wake and fold all our new towels as neatly as I could,
and pile them in high piles so you could see them,
in case there was an emergency.

*

What I didn't like was how people talked to me
now that I was no longer single; they were nicer.

Men who never looked at me would start up a conversation,
like I was suddenly some safer form of fire.

When my dad became a widower, women brought meals,
and wine, and pies.

The word *widower* looks like *window.*

Something you can see yourself in, in the dark.

*

We fell in love around the same time, which seemed right.
And also wrong. Look at us, living!

They met at the same time: his and mine.
I didn't realize it, but I was wearing
my dead stepmom's sunglasses.

His new love was stunning and kind and I tried
to imagine I was seeing her through her eyes,
like looking up from the bottom of a pool.

*

No one wants to be remembered
for their death, or rather,
I don't. So why do I remember hers
and remember hers?

I think I did everything right.

Someone told me that I should have told her all the things
        that she had done to hurt me before she died.

But I didn't. Still, I lost her face.

*

Months later, when we went on our first date, I tried to seem
        put together, I wore a shawl she had given me.
And her ring.

I thought everything was behind me:
death, and dying, and sickness.

I didn't know I was changing my life—
        that I would have done anything,
that what was left of me would become
so ruthless to survive.

IN A MEXICAN RESTAURANT I RECALL
HOW MUCH YOU UPSET ME

Tonight over casual conversation,
words brought you up or out
from where I keep you,
and you were my stepmom again
and I was telling some of his family,
my family now, how it was
to have you as a mother figure
all growing up: you the keeper of lists,
you the flag in the moon, and the moon,
you the garden and the grave,
you who I held as the last air left.
And then you were what? What then?
Oh body where do we keep it?
Oh how I don't offer enough.
In one sentence, in a Mexican restaurant,
you were alive, and then dead again,
and then we had a margarita. That can't be
enough, can it? What do you want me to say?
Sometimes you were mean.
Sometimes I was angry:
you left me when I was 15,
you sent my dog to the pound,
you hung up on my brother.
But love is impossible and it goes on
despite the impossible. You're the muscle
I cut from the bone and still the bone
remembers, still it wants (so much, it wants)

the flesh back, the real thing,
if only to rail against it, if only
to argue and fight, if only to miss
a solve-able absence.

I'm cold in my heart, coal-hard
knot in the mountain buried
deep in the boarded-up mine. So,
I let death in, learn to prospect
the between-dreams of the dying,
the one dream that tells you when
to throw up, the other, when
you're in pain. I tell you
I will love someone that you
will never meet, death's warm
breath at the mouth
of the body's holler.
You are crying in the shower.
I am crying near the shower.
Your body a welcomed-red
fire-starter in steam and I think,
How scared I would be
if I were death. How could I
come to this house, come
to this loved being, see
the mountain's power
and dare blast you down.
I dry you off and think,
if I were death come to take you,
your real-earth explosives,
I would be terrified.

Sun in the cool expressway underpass air
and Ma calls, says it's nice out today
during her long walk through the vineyard
where spring's pushed out every tizzy-tongued
flower known to the valley's bosom of light.
I say, *Look, we're talking about the weather,*
and she says, *You know, it does help you
see the person you're talking to.* (The difference
in a wind-blown winter's walk in January cold
and the loose steps of sun on far-off shoulders.)
Then I say, *Now, we're talking about talking
about the weather. It's very meta of us.*
Yes, she says, *we could go on like this forever.*
And it's been exactly two months since
C died, my hands holding her head, odd
extraordinary February sun gone down
on the smooth slope of green grass, and
all my father and I had done all day was
talk about two things: the weather and her
breathing. (That machine-body gone harsh
in its prolonging and the loud gasping sigh of dying,
thick as a hawk's cry, breaking out in the cloudless
atmosphere.) Some impossibly still moment,
we stood looking at the long field's pull
and we wanted her to die, for her sake,
wanted the motor of body to give up and go.
How strange this silent longing for death,
as if you could make the sun not come up,
the world's wheeling and wheeling its seasons

like a cruel continuation of stubborn force.
But that's not how it happens. Instead, light
escapes from the heart's room and for a moment
you believe the clock will stop itself. Absence.
You see: light escapes from a body at night
and in the morning, despite the oppressive vacancy
of her leaving's shadow, light comes up
over the mountains and it is and it is and it is.

What I didn't say
when she asked me
why I knew so much
about dying was that,
for me, it was work.
When Dad called to say
we had a month, I made a list.
I called in my team
to my office in a high rise,
those Rosies of know-how,
those that had lost someone loved,
those that had done the assembly line
of a home death, and said,
What's this about not keeping
her on TPN? One woman,
who was still soft with sadness,
said, *It depends on whether*
she wants to die of heart failure
or to drown in her own fluids.
I nodded, and wrote that down
like this was a meeting
about a client who wasn't happy.
What about hospice? I asked.
They said, *They'll help,*
but your dad and you guys
will do most of it.
I put a star by that.
We had a plan of action.
When this happens, we do this.

When that happens, we do that.
But what I forgot
was that it was our plan,
not hers, not the one doing the dying,
this was a plan for those
who still had a *next*.
See, our job was simple:
keep on living. Her job was harder,
the hardest. Her job,
her work, was to let the machine
of survival break down,
make the factory fail,
to know that this war was winless,
to know that she would singlehandedly
destroy us all.

I can almost hear the kudzu growing. The rain is hitting the pavement hard, and across the street, in the bunch of tangled woods where I think the owl lives, though I'm not terribly sure, I can hear the kudzu creeping. Is it weird to say that I could hear you dying like that? Slowly, but viciously, inching your way toward the gray sky, tongue out to catch what was left of the world. You floated in the sea for a bit before, swam with the dolphins off the coast before, you drank mai tais before, and smoked pot under a palm tree before, but the before was always that, *the before*. And underneath you could hear it coming, not like a train or something metal, but something clearly unstoppable, and it made a sound, like wet leaves, a weed spreading its runners, stretching out to meet what was next, feeding delightedly, unaware it was about to darken our whole world with its rapid climbing toward the sky.

When she was dying, it was impossible to see forward to the next minute. What was happening—for whole weeks—was all that was happening and happening and happening. Months before that, I got the dumb soup wrong. How awful. It was all she wanted and I had gotten it wrong. Then, in the airless days when it was really happening, we started to power panic that we didn't know enough. What should we do with her ashes? *Water or dirt. Water or dirt.* Once, she asked to just be thrown into the river where we used to go, still alive, but not living anymore. After it was done, I couldn't go back to my life. You understand, right? It wasn't the same. I couldn't tell if I loved myself more or less. It wasn't until later, when I moved in with him and stood outside on our patchy imperfect lawn, that I remembered what had been circling in me: I am beautiful. I am full of love. I am dying.

Careful of what I carry
in my head and in my hollow,

I've been a long time worried
about grasping infinity

and coaxing some calm
out of the softest part

of the pins and needles
of me. I'd like to take a nap.

But not a nap that's eternal,
a nap where you wake up

having dreamt of falling, but
you've only fallen into

an ease so unknown to you
it looks like a new country.

Let me slip into a life less messy.
Let me slip into your sleeve.

Be very brave about my
trespass, the plan is simple—

the plan is the clock tower
and the lost crow. It'll be rich.

We'll live forever. Every moon
will be a moon of surrender

and lemon seeds. You there,
standing up in the crowd,

I'm not proud. The stove
can't boast of the meal.

All this to say—consider this,
with your combination of firefly

and train whistle, consider this,
with your maze and steel,

I want to be the rough clothes
you can't sleep in.

Now, we take the moon
into the middle of our brains

so we look like roadside stray cats
with bright flashlight-white eyes

in our faces, but no real ideas
of when or where to run.

We linger on the field's green edge
and say, *Someday, son, none of this*

will be yours. Miracles are all around.
We're not so much homeless

as we are home-free, penny-poor,
but plenty lucky for love and leaves

that keep breaking the fall. Here it is:
the new way of living with the world

inside of us so we cannot lose it,
and we cannot be lost. You and me

are us and them, and it and sky.
It's hard to believe we didn't

know that before; it's hard to believe
we were so hollowed out, so drained,

only so we could shine a little harder
when the light finally came.

Ma's in the wind-pummeled double-wide
waiting for the retired policemen
to bring their retired police horses
to the ranch. She's at the window now
describing the rain, the two-horse trailer,
and also, how sometimes she and my stepdad
talk about death for a long time.
How imagining death can make it easier
to live and I agree and say, *It's called die
before you die.* What is being delivered
here is a horse who's had a hard life.
A large quarter horse named Seattle—
a horse with a city name who protected a city,
who was spooked outside the baseball stadium
when a shopping bag wrapped around his leg,
a plastic thing versus a muscle-bound animal
in a busy crowd and a flash accident killed
a man. But then, I wonder, what for the horse?
Never to be ridden, stuck numb in a stall,
lightning bugs torturing the poor blood?
I bet that horse might have wanted to
die before he died. But not yet.
What is being delivered here is release.
Today, his officer-rider is finally retired, too,
with an old badge on the dashboard
and a fine plan to drive all the way to Montana,
where the rider has bought a ranch for his horse,
Seattle. The rider and his horse, with his city-name,
and his forgiven city-mistakes, are charting

a clear new territory of absolution, and it makes
Ma and me happy. How good it is to love
live things, even when what they've done
is terrible, how much we each want to be
the pure exonerated creature, to be turned loose
into our own wide open without a single
harness of sin to stop us.

No shoes and a glossy
red helmet, I rode
on the back of my dad's
Harley at seven years old.
Before the divorce.
Before the new apartment.
Before the new marriage.
Before the apple tree.
Before the ceramics in the garbage.
Before the dog's chain.
Before the koi were all eaten
by the crane. Before the road
between us there was the road
beneath us, and I was just
big enough not to let go:
Henno Road, creek just below,
rough wind, chicken legs,
and I never knew survival
was like that. If you live,
you look back and beg
for it again, the hazardous
bliss before you know
what you would miss.

Witness the wet dead snake,
its long hexagonal pattern weaved
around its body like a code for creation,
curled up cold on the newly tarred road.
Let us begin with the snake: the fact
of death, the poverty of place, of skin
and surface. See how the snake is cut
in two—its body divided from its brain.
Imagine now, how it moves still, both
sides, the tail dancing, the head dancing.
Believe it is the mother and the father.
Believe it is the mouth and the words.
Believe it is the sin and the sinner—
the tempting, the taking, the apple, the fall,
every one of us guilty, the story of us all.
But then return to the snake, pitiful dead
thing, forcefully denying the split of its being,
longing for life back as a whole, wanting
you to see it for what it is: something
that loves itself so much it moves across
the boundaries of death to touch itself
once more, to praise both divided sides
equally, as if it was easy.

Nights when it's warm
and no one is watching,
I walk to the edge
of the road and stare
at all the fireflies.
I squint and pretend
they're hallucinations,
bright made-up waves
of the brain.
I call them,
field bling.
I call them,
fancy creepies.
It's been a long time
since I've wanted to die,
it makes me feel
like taking off
my skin suit
and seeing how
my light flies all
on its own, neon
and bouncy like a
wannabe star.

Last night we killed a possum,
out of mercy, in the middle of the road.

It was dying, its face was bloody,
the back legs were shattered. The mistake

I made was getting out of the car
(you told me not to), but I wanted to be

sure, needed to know for sure, that it could
not be saved. (Someone else had hit it.)

The sound it was making. The sound
folded me back into the airless car.

Do it, do it fast, I lowered my head
until the thud was done. You killed it quiet.

We drove home under the sickle moon,
laundry gone cold and dry on the line.

But that was last night. This morning
the sun is coming alive in the kitchen.

You've gone to get us gas station coffee
and there is so much life all over the place.

3

In the black illegible moment of foolish
want, there is also a neon sign flashing,
the sign above the strip joint where my
second big love worked as a bouncer
and saved the girls from unwanted hands,
unpaid-for hands. Thin-lipped ladies
with a lot on their minds and more on
their backs, loaded for bear, and for
the long winter's rain, loaded for real,
and I've always been a jealous girl,
but when he'd come home with a 4 a.m.
stomp in his boots and undress to bed,
he was fully there, fully in the room,
my sleeping body made awake, awake,
and there was a gentleness to this,
a long opening that seemed to join us
in the saddest hour. Before now, I don't
know if I have ever loved anyone, or if
I have ever been loved, but men have
been very good to me, have seen
my absurd out-of-place-ness, my bent
grin and un-called-for loud laugh
and have wanted to love me for it,
have been so warm in their wanting
that sometimes I wanted to love them, too.
And I think that must be worth something,
that it should be a celebrated thing,
that though I have not stood on a mountain
under the usual false archway of tradition

and chosen one person forever, what I have
done is risked everything for that hour,
that hour in the black night, where one
flashing light looks like love, I have
pulled over my body's car and let
myself believe that the dance was
only for me, that this gift of a breathing
one-who-wants was always a gift,
was the only sign worth stopping for,
that the neon glow was a real star,
gleaming in its dying, like us all,
like us all.

After we tumbled and fought and tumbled again,
he and I sat out in the backyard before his parents
came home, flushed and flowered and buzzing
with the quickening ripples of blood growing up
and I could barely feel my hands, my limbs numbed
from the new touching that seemed strikingly
natural but also painfully kindled in the body's stove.
Oh my newness! Oh my new obsession, his hands!
I thought I could die and be happy and be humbled
by luck of a first love and a first full-fledged fuck.
I wanted to tell my ma. I wanted to make a movie.
I wanted to blast out of my bare feet to sky-town
as we passed the joint in the soupy summer's air
too-spiced with oak leaves, eucalyptus, and smoke.
I thought I might have a heart attack, kind of craved
one, kind of wanted the bum-rush of goodbye
like every kid wants when they're finally on fire.
Then, out of the stoned-breath quiet of the hills,
came another animal, a real animal, a wandering
madrone-skinned horse from the neighbor's garden,
bowed-back, higher than a man's hat, high up
and hitched to nothing. He rustled down his giant
head to where we sat, baked and big-eyed at this
animal come to greet us in our young afterglow.
He seemed almost worthy of complete devotion.
We rubbed his long horse nose, his marble eyes turning
to take us all in, to inhale us, to accept our now-selves
and he was older, a wise, hoofed, grizzled, equine elder
and I thought, this was what it was to be blessed—

to know a love that was beyond an owning, beyond
the body and its needs, but went straight from wild
thing to wild thing, approving of its wildness.

The strange crying sounds
of the peacocks on the private
school grounds echo on perfect
lawns, and I remember the unruly
feathered fowl of my earlier years
that draped the flimflam landscape
of the home of the first girl I ever kissed.
The students today make a vow
of silence to honor gay and lesbian kids
who've been bullied, so when we visit
and read poems, they can't speak,
they are silent for those that are silenced.
And I'm thinking now of making out
with Sarah, and how later we made
pickle and mayonnaise sandwiches
and sat by the edge of her empty pool—
our legs swinging into nothingness,
the sun's heat at our backs, the sounds
of peacocks screaming, at first harmless,
then like some far-off siren.

Valencia in the nineties, nowhere
were the oranges, except one slight
site from the train's blur. I burnt
my nipples right off the bat. No way
you could be as pretty as the girls
in Valencia, topless and tanned
all over. Pale blue hostel sheets
were barely bearable. All night
I thought I'd die when the moon
came in and I'd wake to the pinching
skin. But I didn't die. I went right
back the next day, but in a t-shirt
and didn't try to be pretty, just
swam like something ordinary,
something worthy of the sea.

Up above a bar in their first apartment,
my ma and my dad are in some whorl
of late '60s haze in the Castro District
of San Francisco where the jukebox
below played the same Frankie Valli song,
Sherry, Sherry baby, Sherry, Sherry baby
until they go almost mad with their
paper floors and cheap wall hangings
swinging in the falsetto of the city's
changing swirl of hips and hopes
and I love them so. She's in the window
crying because the city is too big, and also
because we are at war, and he goes to work
in tough schools that need teachers,
Spanish-speaking teachers not scared of much
except how to make rent and make the world maybe
better or easier or livable. Nights, they get stoned
in small apartments and eat enchiladas
in the warm corn-filled kitchens
and she's going to paint and have big ideas,
and he's going to save the world with curriculum,
and no one knows how much that want matters,
how much the ordinary need to make some real life
was enough to give them the drive to make
some real nice mistakes. How years later,
some might say that their love was not a love,
or was not the right kind of love, but rather
a sort of holding on in order to escape another
trapped fate of desert heat and parental push,

but I want to tell you, nothing was an accident.
Not their innocence or their ideals, not their
selfish need, not their dark immortal laughter,
not the small place with the roaring traffic, not
the bus rides, or riots, or carelessness and calm,
not the world that wanted them in it, that needed
their small, young faces united in kiss and weep,
not the song that surrounded them in a good fight,
that repeated, *Come, come, come out tonight.*

In this, the current recasting of the great plummet,
it is I, and not the other grand-eyed cows off Leveroni Road,
who watches the two cloudy youths climb into the backseat
of the long boat-like car during the plunging dark hour
of no turning back. I am not folded into its tongue-red
interior watching the headlights of the passing traffic
trance the windows like far-off lighthouse lights pulsing
at us, lost in our swollen inky sea. In this version, I am
the still bovine beauty staring into Carriger Creek, hungry
for nothing but what comes every day: grass and sky,
and the silvery creek water reflecting the grass and sky.
By the bend in the clean zipper of stream, by the gate
of my life, a metal animal's insides steam up and I understand—
so many dolorous selves in each of us dissolving into fog.

My ex got hit by a bus.

He wrote me in a text to tell me this.
　　Now will you talk to me? I got hit by a bus.

He even sent me a link to the blurry footage on the news.
I never wanted to see him come to harm, or watch it.

Oh maybe a little cockroach infestation.
　　Little aliens all over the clean, misleading counters of his life.

My ex, a few exes before that, died
　　of a heroin overdose.

After someone hurts you, it's easy to imagine
him fading into the background of the bad film's revenge plot.

It's the joke, right? *I hope you get hit by a bus.*
　　　　I swear I never thought it. No seed of transportation deviance.
No tampering with the great universal brake wires.

I wanted this rusty mailbox,
out here in the boondocks, this man, and this dog,
a little money now and again, some good news.

I'm the hidden bug in the tall weeds,
lighting fires no one can see.

*

When we moved out here together, I kept apologizing
for everything, like a poor orphan in the film about my shame.

He had to tell me to stop. And for days, (maybe weeks?)
I'd hear it in my mind and have to hold it there,
stuck like a cockroach under a glass,
waiting for someone braver to kill it.

Mostly, I enjoy my failings. Until I don't.

In the text from my ex about the bus, he sounds almost funny.
            Like isn't it ironic that I got hit by a bus, when all I ever
                    wanted was to
disappear without a trace.

*

When the plane went down in San Francisco,
I thought of my friend M. He's obsessed with plane crashes.

He memorizes the wrecked metal details,
        the clear cool skies cut by black scars of smoke.

Once, while driving, he told me about all the crashes:
The one in blue Kentucky, in yellow Iowa.

How people go on, and how people don't.

It was almost a year before I learned
that his brother was a pilot.

I can't help it,
I love the way men love.

*

I used to pretend a lot. I'm very good at it.

I bought a creamy corn-colored rotary phone
and I was so fabulous.

I'd sit and tell you about my phone, but the truth was
        it didn't work very well. It made me not want to talk to anyone,
but rather be in a picture, holding the phone, pretending to talk.

That's not unlike some of the people I have claimed to love.

I'd rather tell you about them, stranger, in hot words
        than tug the cold satellites closer for warmth.

*

I imagine the insides of myself sometimes—
        part female, part male, part terrible dragon.

What I saw in the men who came before,
        sometimes I don't want to say this out loud,

was someone I could hold up to my ear
and hear the ocean, something I could say my name into,
and have it returned in the inky waves.

*

Why are we forced into such small spaces together?
        This life in a seedpod.

I remember once, my ex and I, driving in his van.
He pointed out his ex-wife walking.

She looked like me—not her blue hat, or her smallness,
but how deliberately she was walking away from the speeding vehicle.

Now, there's a twisty summer storm outside,
and I desire nothing but this storm to come.

The calm voice on the TV tells us to stay safe.
Says, *Stay safe and seek shelter.*

Somewhere outside of Albuquerque, I was all
fed up with the stories about your ex-girlfriend's
Guess billboard in New York City, and to make
matters worse, I had to pee like a racehorse, or
like a girl who'd had too much to drink way
too far away from home. You stopped at a friend's
body shop to talk about a buddy who was stuck
someplace in Mexico. You were talking, pulling
strings and taking pulls off a brown bottle, and no
one told me where the restroom was, so I walked
back to where the hotrods were displayed like dogs
ready for a fight, baring their grills like teeth.
I was hungry, the air smelled like hot gasoline
and that sweet carnation smell of oil and coolant.
A girl pit bull came and circled me as I circled
the cars; she sniffed my ankles like I was her kin
or on some kind of rescue mission. You were still
talking, not a glance in the direction of me
and the bitch working our ways around
the souped-up Corvettes and the power tools.
The pit was glossy, well cared for, a queen
of the car shop, and when she widened
her hind legs and squatted to pee all over
one of the car's dropped canvases, I took it
as a challenge. That strong yellow stream seemed
to be saying, *Girl, no one's going to tell me*
when to take a leak, when to bow down,
when not to bite. So, right then, in the dim lights
of the strange garage, I lifted my skirt and pissed
like the hard bitch I was.

THE PLUNGE

I bet the steady well never complains
about all the flash dipping in, coins,
coins, and more coins. This life is a fist
of fast wishes caught by nothing
but the fishhook of tomorrow's tug.
I shoved my money in the water once,
threw it like a guaranteed ticket to cash;
it never came true, not the wish,
nor the towering person I was bound to be.
But the back-of-the-throat thrill was real,
when the surface's shine broke. It was enough
to go back again and again, and throw
my whole jonesing body in.

What's the real story?

I had to hurt someone. A woman.

I had to hurt someone who had loved
him before I did, 6 years earlier.

I had to do it with a knife in my teeth.

[Pulls out the knife, turns it in her palms.]

My knife said, *I'm so sorry,* and *I love you,*
and *Please understand.* And *You're married.*
And *Give me this.*

How did you do it?

I crawled on my hands and knees,
and there were dead bodies on the rocks,
all over the rocks, on the red rocks,
picked apart by the seagulls, and I didn't care.

And before?

We were friends. Close.

[Looks out the window, watches storm.]

Maybe I've done it before; maybe I've hurt a woman
and maybe it's fitting that I'd be the low ugly
alive thing doing my living all over the place.

You knew it would hurt her?

Yes and I knew there would be bodies.
Yes and I knew that I'd lose her forever.
Yes and I chose that and I chose to lose her.

How do you love?

Like a fist. Like a knife.
But I want to be more like a weed,
a small frog trembling in air.

[Cries a little.]

Did you live?

Even better, I lived. Even more, I lived.
Even better, I am living.

And fear?

I'm not afraid of hate anymore.
What do we do with grief? Lug it; lug it.

I would do it again.

And later?

I had to come to terms
with how they loved, that they loved.

I couldn't cut it out of me.

And now?

I thought after the first stab, I'd learn to take it,
but even now, I hold the hot blade in the mouth
in case anyone comes to destroy the bloom.

[Puts the knife in her teeth.]

See? The knife I carry?
It cuts my smile even wider.

Some blur of a bird makes
a kid-like laugh out of sea air
and we, heart-hardy, kick
a crack-up back at it like
the opposite of throwing stones.
Like releasing tiny hot air
balloons up, moon-bound
and hell-bent on defying
the usual gravity of this spin.
Sky, here, we toss a bone
into your open endlessness,
the sound of crackle, a timbre
of animal-warmth. Oh let us be
a bird flying wholly for the sake
of flying, to be that breath-
machine that even the anchored
earth-bound wavers want
to root for, want to look up
and say, *Rally, rally, win.*

The sun is still down and maybe even downer.
Two owls, one white and one large-eared,
dive into a nothingness that is a field, night-beast
in the swoop-down, (the way we all have to
make a living). Let's be owls tonight, stay up
in the branches of ourselves, wide-eyed,
perched on the edge of euphoric plummet.
All your excellences are making me mouse,
but I will shush and remain the quiet flyer,
the one warm beast still coming to you in the dark
despite all those old, cold, claustrophobic stars.

Late night in a honky-tonk, fried pickles
in a red plastic basket, and it was all Loretta
on the heel-bruised stage, sung by a big girl
we kind of both had a crush on. Nashville
got the best of us, in a bar shootin' Fireball
with the band that just roused the Ryman.
Good grief we were loaded, shotguns,
and the soft-hearted. It's like this:
sometimes the buried buzz comes back,
and soon the kid that cut the lunch line
ain't nothing; and the cruel tongues licking
your insides are gone; the bully girl who
kicked you out of the city is no one, no rotten
crumb left, just a dizzy river of nonsense
in the waxy light under the bright signs and
look here, I won't deny it: I was there,
standing in the bar's bathroom mirror,
saying my name like I was somebody.

We were crossing the headwaters of
the Susquehanna River in our new car
we didn't quite have the money for
but it was slick and silver and we named it
after the local strip club next to the car wash:
The Spearmint Rhino, and this wasn't long
after your mother said she wasn't sure
if one of your ancestors died in childbirth
or was struck by lightning, there just wasn't
anyone left to set the story straight, and we
started to feel old. And it snowed. The ice
and salt and mud on the car made it look
like how we felt on the inside. The dog
was asleep on my lap. We had seven more hours
before our bed in the bluegrass would greet us
like some southern cousin we forgot we had.
Sometimes, you have to look around
at the life you've made and sort of nod at it,
like someone moving their head up and down
to a tune they like. New York City seemed years
away and all the radio stations had unfamiliar
call letters and talked about God, the one
that starts his name with a capital and wants
you not to get so naked all the time.
Sometimes, there seems to be a halfway point
between where you've been and everywhere
else, and we were there. All the trees were dead,
and the hills looked flat like in real bad landscape
paintings in some nowhere gallery off an interstate

but still, it looked kind of pretty. Not because
of the snow, but because you somehow found
a decent song on the dial and there you were,
with your marvelous mouth, singing full-lunged,
driving full-speed into the gloomy thunderhead,
glittery and blazing and alive. And it didn't matter
what was beyond us, or what came before us,
or what town we lived in, or where the money came from,
or what new night might leave us hungry and reeling,
we were simply going forward, riotous and windswept,
and all too willing to be struck by something shining
and mad, and so furiously hot it could kill us.

4

It was, for a time, a loud twittering flight
of psychedelic-colored canaries: a cloud
of startle and get-out in the ornamental
irons of the rib cage. Nights when the moon
was wide like the great eye of a universal
beast coming close for a kill, it was a cave
of bitten bones and snake skins, eggshell dust,
and charred scraps of a frozen-over flame.
All the things it has been: kitchen knife
and the ancient carp's frown, cavern of rust
and worms in the airless tire swing,
cactus barb, cut-down tree, dead cat
in the plastic crate. Still, how the great middle
ticker marched on, and from all its four chambers
to all its forgiveness, unlocked the sternum's
door, reversed and reshaped until it was a new
bright carnal species, more accustomed to grief,
and ecstatic at the sight of you.

It's a day when all the dogs of all
the borrowed houses are angel-footing
down the hard hardwood of middle-America's
newly loaned-up renovated kitchen floors,
and the world's nicest pie I know
is somewhere waiting for the right
time to offer itself to the wayward
and the word-weary. How come the road
goes coast to coast and never just
dumps us in the water, clean and
come clean, like a fish slipped out
of the national net of *longing for joy.*
How come it doesn't? On a road trip
through the country, someone saw
a waitress who walked in the train's
diner car and swished her non-aproned
end and said, *Hot stuff and food too.*
My family still says it, when the food is hot,
and the mood is good inside the open windows.
I'd like to wear an apron for you
and come over with non-church sanctioned
knee-highs and the prettiest pie of birds
and ocean water and grief. I'd like
to be younger when I do this, like the country
before Mr. Meriwether rowed the river
and then let the country fill him up
till it killed him hard by his own hand.
I'd like to be that dog they took with them,

large and dark and silent and un-blamable.
Or I'd like to be Emily Dickinson's dog, Carlo,
and go on loving the rare un-loveable puzzle
of woman and human and mind. But
I bet I'm more the house beagle and the howl
and the obedient eyes of everyone wanting
to make their own kind of America,
but still be America, too. The road is long
and all the dogs don't care too much
about roadside concrete history and postcards
of state treasures, they just want their head
out the window, and the speeding air to make them
feel faster and younger, and newer than all the dogs
that went before them, they want to be your only dog,
your best-loved dog, for the good dog of today
to be the only beast that matters.

My older brother says he doesn't consider himself Latino anymore and I understand what he means, but I stare at the weird fruit in my hand and wonder what it is to lose a spiny layer. He's explaining how white and lower-middle class we grew up and how we don't know anything about any culture except maybe Northern California culture, which means we get stoned more often and frown on super stores. I want to do whatever he says. I want to be something entirely without words. I want to be without tongue or temper. Two days ago in Tennessee someone said, *Stop it, Ada's Mexican*. And I didn't know what they were talking about until one of them said, *At least I didn't say wetback*. And everyone laughed. Honestly, another drink and I could have hit someone. Started the night's final fight. And I don't care what he says. My brother would have gone down swinging and fought off every redneck whitey in the room.

I don't even know how to get to Alaska,
or how to talk about race when the original tongue is gone.

Imagine a woman at the edge, at the border
      of the universe waving without an idea
      of where to wave, into emptiness, into a bliss?

I moved to New York City once with cash money
I'd saved from being a receptionist for the county and a box
      of books I'd never read.

      No one tells you how old you'll be one day, or rather,
no one can tell you. Generations are forgotten with their real letters.

Right now, he is trying to explain to me
why whales don't get dizzy, something
        about the caves of the inner ear,

but all I see is this spinning, icy black water,
enormous rush, mammalian greatness beneath me,

and how maybe I could swim to Alaska?

I heard about a woman once, maybe she was my mother,
      who wanted to move to Alaska, but the bears were trouble.

They gave her a goat to take to the outhouse.

      (Not for protection, but for offering.)

It had a little gold bell, the goat,
that rang out in the air like a cannon.

I still worry, even now, about the goat.
Did it know what its job was? Ringing on like that?

I prefer not to make a sound. Will the idea of race go away
        if we all stop talking?

No, we require the goat.

We send people before us, scouts
of air, of water, of fire, of earth,
to tell us how to live.

I want to be the largest animal that ever existed.
The one blue mother—
I'd save the goat, and the bear.

        Did you know giant whales have a spindle cell
        making them capable of attachment
        and of great suffering?

I want to ride around gently and wave
        at the colorful human parade, especially at you,
but in the end I want the watery under.

Evolution, of course.

(Don't think of the trash the size of Texas.)

Did you know that whales returned to the water?
   It went like this: water, land, water. Like a waltz.

I once had a record of whale sounds,
   I swear I understood.

It didn't matter what worlds they were under,
   what language,
   what depth of water divided,
   the song went on and on.

What I mean is: none of this is chaos.
Immigration, cross the river, the blood of us.
   It goes like this: water, land, water. Like a waltz.

I am in no hurry to stop believing we are supposed
to sway like this, that we too are immense and calling out.

After Jose Dávila's cut-outs and for Francisco Carlos Limón

Where do you keep your sharp tools of history?
Shattered black spikes wedged in the rigid spine?

What did the spikes hold up? Whose puny flag?
When was the border just a line in the dirt?

Whose dirt? Whose line? Where do the ghosts
go when we refuse to spit out their clouds?

It's true, he smudged oranges in Canoga Park
and lived in a chicken coop, yes, oranges.

Now, there are no oranges at all in the whole
of San Fernando Valley, no oranges, just names

of streets: Orange Boulevard, Orange County.
The way we do. Naming what's no longer there.

Here was an orange grove; here was a brown boy.
I bow down, in my suit of hand-me-down spikes,

into the coop where the warm fowl slept against him.
The hens do not love him. Neither do the oranges.

But they survive together: fuel for the future:

A picture of a feather without the bird,
A picture of an orange without the tree,
A picture of a shadow without a boy.

TATTOO THEORY

For Michael & Adam

My own personal map of America on the back of the airplane seat where the cartoon plane tells you where you've been and where you're going, is, for some reason, in Spanish. So it reads *Montes Apalaches*. And I like the way it sounds. But the shape of Nebraska is still the same despite the translation; it looks like a sad animal with his head hangdog low. Just countable days ago, we drove through that glum dog place and the boys wanted tattoos of the state's outline. *Nebraska! Nebraska Forever! Yeah*! I love the keeping of it, the wanting to keep it, but maybe not on my body. What if I love another state more? What if I love the *Montes Apalaches?* What if I stop remembering? What if here's where I want to keep it? Here's my permanent puncture, here's my unstoppable ink.

THE PROBLEM WITH TRAVEL

Every time I'm in an airport,
I think I should drastically
change my life: Kill the kid stuff,
start to act my numbers, set fire
to the clutter and creep below
the radar like an escaped canine
sneaking along the fence line.
I'd be cable-knitted to the hilt,
beautiful beyond buying, believe in
the maker and fix my problems
with prayer and property.
Then, I think of you, home
with the dog, the field full
of purple pop-ups—we're small and
flawed, but I want to be
who I am, going where
I'm going, all over again.

Big blue horizon wakes me
from a car catnap and the boys
tell me about Boston, the bombs.
Soft edges of sleep turn sharp
and point inward to the terrified
heart. Out the window, ancient
horses and trees bent over
like the wisest crones. Under
the overpass a flittering swarm
of mud swallows have built
careful nests with prairie clay.
How do they do it? Demand the
sweet continuance of birth and flight
in a place so utterly reckless? How
masterful and mad is hope.

That we might walk out into the woods
together, and afterwards make toast
in our sock feet, still damp from the fern's
wet grasp, the spiky needles stuck to our
legs, that's all I wanted, the dog in the mix,
jam sometimes, but not always. But somehow,
I've stopped praising you. How the valley
when you first see it—the small roads back
to your youth—is so painfully pretty at first,
then, after a month of black coffee, it's just
another place your bullish brain exists, bothered
by itself and how hurtful human life can be.
Isn't that how it is? You wake up some days
full of crow and shine, and then someone
has put engine coolant in the medicine
on another continent and not even crying
helps cure the idea of purposeful poison.
What kind of woman am I? What kind of man?
I'm thinking of the way my stepdad got sober,
how he never told us, just stopped drinking
and sat for a long time in the low folding chair
on the Bermuda grass reading and sometimes
soaking up the sun like he was the story's only
subject. When he drove me to school, we decided
it would be a good day if we saw the blue heron
in the algae-covered pond next to the road,
so that if we didn't see it, I'd be upset. Then,
he began to lie. To tell me he'd seen it when
he hadn't, or to suppose that it had just

taken off when we rounded the corner in
the gray car that somehow still ran, and I
would lie, too, for him. I'd say I saw it.
Heard the whoosh of wings over us.
That's the real truth. What we told each other
to help us through the day: the great blue heron
was there, even when the pond dried up,
or froze over; it was there because it had to be.
Just now, I felt like I wanted to be alone
for a long time, in a folding chair on the lawn
with all my private agonies, but then I saw you
and the way you're hunching over your work
like a puzzle, and I think even if I fail at everything,
I still want to point out the heron like I was taught,
still want to slow the car down to see the thing
that makes it all better, the invisible gift, what
we see when we stare long enough into nothing.

I lied about the whales. Fantastical blue
water-dwellers, big, slow moaners of the coastal.
I never saw them. Not once that whole frozen year.
Sure, I saw the raw white gannets hit the waves
so hard it could have been a showy blow hole.
But I knew it wasn't. Sometimes, you just want
something so hard you have to lie about it,
so you can hold it in your mouth for a minute,
how real hunger has a real taste. Someone once
told me gannets, those voracious sea birds
of the North Atlantic chill, go blind from the height
and speed of their dives. But that, too, is a lie.
Gannets never go blind and they certainly never die.

Even the grass
smells like horses
that smell like
sex and sweat,
and it makes
the whole day
feel sticky wet
with what's next.
He's betting
in the living room,
which T calls
the drinks room,
and I don't know
if I'm made up
of mama material.
The race goes off.
I take the dog out
so I can't hear
who wins. Either
money or none,
but we'll still be
animals shoving
our bodies in air,
racing no one
but ourselves,
the grass thick
and trembling
at our speed.

—After "The Wreck of the Hesperus"
by Henry Wadsworth Longfellow

There is a spreading frost
        trilling its white agony on the inside of the window,

where my guitar has been frozen for days,
                        the heated song gone out of the instrument.

Let me start here: I am as cold as I have ever been.

Two days ago, a week? A mythic wreck came—
                        such was the wreck of the two of us.

I'm such an ignorant boat—
        a lost sea-tossed daughter   pierced by time's spiked icicles,

begging for the original mouth's thawing water.

Isn't it funny? How the cold numbs everything   but grief.
If we could light up the room with pain,
                        we'd be such a   glorious fire.

Clock: turn back, turn back—
                everything you've dialed to black.

What was it I wanted?
        The captain to sail safely? To land alive and, like survival, loved?

But *colder and louder blew the wind.*

And still there were books to read, and dishes, the dog's needy tongue.

What good is bravery—
                        on the rocks and the hard sea-sand?

If I can have a child. If I cannot have a child. If you do not care.

I am gleaming. Promise you'll see me gleam.

Crowned newly with a fearsome cutting,
I fold the aqua blanket twice to stay alive.

Headstones in the heart's holler, sludge
of what's left after the mountain's blasted.

Not a kid anymore, there are no pretty victims
or greasy cavernous villains spitting blazes.

Just a week ago, I wondered what this, this,
would be like, to be wholly blown apart.

The women of Appalachia are watching
each home poisoned by bad air, deadly water,

their kin are losing teeth. Liver cancer,
gallbladders full of black coal sludge, and still

they stand for the mountains they loved, rage
in the coal muck for their blood-deep origin.

What must it be like, I wonder, to fear the fall
every day? Might come a flood. Might come death.

To look out at the coal fires burning
every hour endlessly for fifty years and to know

your land may be condemned, razed, and not want
to simply lie down and die. I am not that strong.

Wickedness has leaked into the home I made,
and I want to burn it down. Sister, tell me

how you stand the murderous fury. You there
still singing, I crave demolishing, to eat explosives.

How could I have imagined this? Mortal me,
brutal disaster born out of so much greed.

I point out the ice on the power lines,
dripping wet into clean frozen plumes.

Look how solid, how still (oh us!)
in the swinging blast of this epic chill,

and yet, we both know they crack,
(don't we?) break, drip, give up, crash, come

down and turn to earth again. Gone
the sparkle, the dazzling spike of shiver

that threatens to stick around forever,
like agony. I want to see it die: unfriendly

numbness. The largeness in me, the hot
gore of my want and want, wants to disarm

the fixedness of this. I'll be the strike anywhere,
the reckless match you can count on

to claim a life, or to save one.

Nights, I wonder about the sanity of Icarus,
wax and wings both wasted on the sun's scorch.

If I'd a handmade, fanned out, feathered set, me?
I'd choose the moon, always the sister moon.

Cold, comely queen of the sky. Pockmarked
with craters, pummeled by meteors and still

shining. Imagine, the gathering on the shore,
you, holding my coat for a warm come-back.

We mean a thing is impossible when we say
we're shooting for that great orbital puller.

How hard can you glow? asks the owl's eye.
What radiant part of you wishes to dynamite?

I used to think it was like a light bulb, life,
dangling in the chest, asking to be switched on.

But it's not the light that's ever in question,
rather, what's your brilliant, glaring wattage?

What do you dare to gleam out and reflect?
If I were to fall (sabotaged wax, torn pinion),

I'd want to fall from the terrifying height
of her, the dust of my years crazy and flashing

lit up by the victory of my disastrous flight.

Say tomorrow doesn't come.
Say the moon becomes an icy pit.
Say the sweet-gum tree is petrified.
Say the sun's a foul black tire fire.
Say the owl's eyes are pinpricks.
Say the raccoon's a hot tar stain.
Say the shirt's plastic ditch-litter
Say the kitchen's a cow's corpse.
Say we never get to see it: bright
future, stuck like a bum star, never
coming close, never dazzling.
Say we never meet her. Never him.
Say we spend our last moments staring
at each other, hands knotted together,
clutching the dog, watching the sky burn.
Say, *It doesn't matter.* Say, *That would be
enough.* Say you'd still want this: us alive,
right here, feeling lucky.

ACKNOWLEDGMENTS

My gratitude goes to the editors of the following journals, in which the poems in this book, sometimes in earlier versions, first appeared:

American Poetry Review: "The Rewilding" and "Home Fires"

Buenos Aires Review: "The Problem with Travel" and "Accident Report in the Tall, Tall Weeds"

Catch Up: "During the Impossible Age of Everyone" and "In the Country of Resurrection"

Compose: "We Are Surprised," "The Noisiness of Sleep," and "Torn"

Conduit: "Relentless"

Connotations Press: "The Wild Divine," "The Long Ride," and "Play It Again"

Copper Nickel: "The Whale and the Waltz Inside of It"

Descant: "The Quiet Machine," "Day of Song, Day of Silence," "Lashed to the Helm, All Stiff and Stark," "The Vine," and "Miracle Fish"

Dream the End: "Someplace Like Montana"

Guernica: "Downhearted"

Gulf Coast: "How to Triumph Like a Girl" and "Down Here"

Hell Yes Press, 21 Love Poems Mix-tape: "Oh Please, Let It Be Lightning"

Hick Poetics Anthology: "Field Bling"

Los Angeles Review of Books: "Call to Post" and "Long Ago & the Cow Comes Back"

Luminosity Project (Lexington Arts League Commission): "The Other Wish"

Poecology: "What it Looks Like to Us and the Words We Use"

Poem-A-Day, Poets.org: "Roadside Attractions with the Dogs of America," "The Conditional," and "Before"

Poetry Daily: "Tattoo Theory"

Provincetown Arts: "Mowing"

The New Yorker: "State Bird"

New York Times: "Oranges & the Ocean"

Thrush Poetry Journal: "The Tree of Fire," "The Saving Tree," "Drift," and "Cower"

TriQuarterly Online: "In a Mexican Restaurant I Recall How Much You Upset Me" and "Tattoo Theory"

The Tusculum Review: "Glow"

Two Bridges Review: "How Far Away We Are" and "I Remember the Carrots"

Typo: "The Last Move"

Waxwing: "After You Toss Around the Ashes," "Prickly Pear & Fisticuffs," and "The Riveter"

ZYZZYVA: "Midnight, Talking About Our Exes"

The poem "How to Triumph Like a Girl" was awarded the Pushcart Prize (2015).

The poem "What It Looks Like to Us and the Words We Use" was chosen by Ted Kooser for his newsletter, *American Life in Poetry.*

I am beyond grateful for the advice and support of my teachers, friends, and family who made this book (and life) possible. I'd especially like to thank those people who consistently read my poems before they are even poems: Brady T. Brady, Stacia Brady, Jennifer L. Knox, Jason Schneiderman, Adam Clay, Michael Robins, Alex Lemon, Trish Harnetiaux, and Heather Grossmann. Giant thanks also goes to Diana Lee Craig and Jeff Baker who gave me a place on the mountain to write. And to my father whose constant love and support have given me the permission to write. To the good folks at Milkweed Editions and my editor, Wayne Miller, you are a light in a storm. And to Lucas & Lily Bean, we dream as a team.

JUDE DOMSKI

ADA LIMÓN is the twenty-fourth U.S. Poet Laureate as well as the author of *The Hurting Kind* and five other collections of poems. These include, most recently, *The Carrying*, which won the National Book Critics Circle Award and was named a finalist for the PEN/ Jean Stein Book Award, and *Bright Dead Things*, which was named a finalist for the National Book Award, the National Book Critics Circle Award, and the Kingsley Tufts Award. Limón is a recipient of a Guggenheim Fellowship, and her work has appeared in the *New Yorker*, the *New York Times*, and *American Poetry Review*, among others. She is the host of American Public Media's weekday poetry podcast *The Slowdown*. Born and raised in California, she now lives in Lexington, Kentucky.

Interior design and typesetting by Gretchen Achilles/WavetrapDesign

Typeset in Adobe Garamond

milkweed
EDITIONS

Founded as a nonprofit organization in 1980, Milkweed Editions is an independent publisher. Our mission is to identify, nurture and publish transformative literature, and build an engaged community around it.

Milkweed Editions is based in Bdé Óta Othúŋwe (Minneapolis) within Mní Sota Makhočhe, the traditional homeland of the Dakhóta people. Residing here since time immemorial, Dakhóta people still call Mní Sota Makhočhe home, with four federally recognized Dakhóta nations and many more Dakhóta people residing in what is now the state of Minnesota. Due to continued legacies of colonization, genocide, and forced removal, generations of Dakhóta people remain disenfranchised from their traditional homeland. Presently, Mní Sota Makhočhe has become a refuge and home for many Indigenous nations and peoples, including seven federally recognized Ojibwe nations. We humbly encourage our readers to reflect upon the historical legacies held in the lands they occupy.

milkweed.org